8/11

AR PTS: 1.0

Were Potato Chips Really Invented by an Angry Chef?

And Other Questions about Food

DEBORAH KOPS

ILLUSTRATIONS BY COLIN W. THOMPSON

LERNER PUBLICATIONS COMPANY

Minneapolis

Contents

Perhaps you've heard beliefs like these about food:

Turkey makes you sleepy!
Fats are always bad for you!

But are these beliefs true? Is there anything to the stories you've heard? Come along with us as we explore the world of food. Find out whether our perceptions about food are

FACT OR FICTION!

Did People in Medieval Europe Really Use Spices to Hide the Smell of Bad Food?

NOPE. But a lot of people think they did.

Here's why. In the Middle Ages (about A.D. 500 to 1500), people had no refrigerators. In fact, they had no electricity at all. And sometimes their meat began to smell pretty awful before they had a chance to cook it. Spices like pepper, nutmeg, and cloves have a much nicer smell. So it makes sense to believe that medieval cooks in Europe added spices to their meat.

But most cooks in the Middle Ages didn't use a lot of spices. There was one simple reason. Spices were too expensive. The spices came from the southern and southeastern parts of Asia, thousands of miles away. One trader in Asia sold the spices to another trader who lived farther west. That trader sold the spices to someone else who lived closer to Europe. By the time the spices finally arrived in European cities and towns, they had been bought and sold many times. And each time, the price of the spices went up. So only wealthy people could afford to eat spiced meat.

People did take steps to keep meat from spoiling in the first place. They covered raw meat with salt. Or they added lots of salt to a liquid and soaked the meat in it.

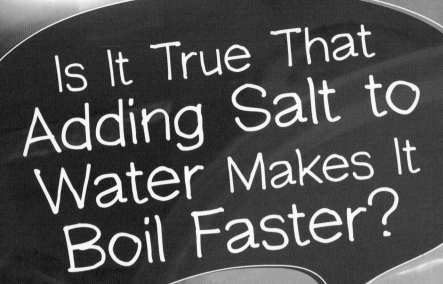

Is It True That Adding Salt to Water Makes It Boil Faster?

NO. Lots of people say it does. But actually, adding salt slows the boiling process.

Why? Well, a pot of water consists of many water molecules (right). (A molecule is the smallest part of a substance that has all the traits of that substance.) Water molecules are so small that you can only see them with a microscope. As water boils, the molecules at the bottom of the pan, closest to the heat source, reach the boiling point. They change to water vapor (the gas form of water). Gases are lighter than liquids such as water. So bubbles of vapor rise to the surface of the water in the pot. That's why you see bubbles when water boils.

A water molecule is made of two parts hydrogen (H) and one part oxygen (O).

When you add salt to water, the salt dissolves, or breaks up in the liquid. And those tiny bits of salt get in the way of the water turning to vapor. So the water takes longer to boil. The salt also absorbs some of the heat energy from the stove. That slows down the boiling too. In fact, anything that dissolves in water—including sugar—slows down boiling.

Did You Know?

The higher up you are, the faster you can boil water. In Miami, Florida, and other places that are close to sea level, water boils when the temperature of the water reaches 212°F (100°C). But in Denver, Colorado, water boils at 196°F (91°C). Denver is 1 mile (1.6 kilometers) above sea level. The pressure of the air is lower at that height. This makes water reach its boiling point faster. That may sound like an advantage. But since the water doesn't get as hot, cooking things in the boiling water actually takes longer.

Do People Really Eat Butterflies and Little Tongues and Ears?

YES. And with the right sauce, they are mighty tasty. But hold on! We're not talking about a gross-out meal. *Linguine* (little tongues), *farfalle* (butterflies), and *orecchiette* (little ears) are the Italian names for three different shapes of pasta.

Linguine are long noodles, like spaghetti but flatter and wider. Farfalle look like butterflies as well as bows. And if you don't want to think of ears while you eat some chewy orecchiette, that's OK. They resemble shells too.

Italians enjoy hundreds of pasta shapes. Over time, Italians have given these shapes playful names. The pasta called "eyes of a sparrow" is like a tiny doughnut. "Little worms" look like thin spaghetti. Angel hair is the thinnest spaghetti of all.

Pasta makers in Italy have also taken their inspiration from industry. The result? Pasta dough has been shaped into "little wheels," "radiators," and "propellers."

This chef is making ravioli. Most pasta starts out as long sheets of rolled-out dough. Then the chef makes it into the shape she wants.

Italians have been eating pasta for centuries. No one is sure exactly when they began turning flour, water, and salt into butterflies and angel hair. But food historians are sure about one thing: Marco Polo, the great explorer from Venice, did not introduce pasta to Italians. Many people wrongly believe that Italian pasta was born after Polo discovered noodles on a trip to China. Marco Polo returned to Italy from China in 1295. However, Italians were eating pasta before that date.

Were Potato Chips Really Invented by an Angry Chef?

THEY WERE!

In 1853 George Crum was working as the chef at a resort in Saratoga Springs, New York. One day, a customer complained that Crum's french fries were too thick and soggy. Crum got mad. He made another batch of fries, but he made them differently. He cut the raw potatoes into very thin slices. Then he fried them in oil until they became really crisp. And he sprinkled them with a lot of salt. That customer was going to wish he hadn't complained, Crum thought.

But Crum was wrong. The customer loved those crispy potatoes. He ordered more. And he told Crum he ought to open his own restaurant. Crum did just that. People lined up to get a seat at his new restaurant. Everyone wanted to try his crunchy potato snack.

Chef George Crum

About seventy years later, someone else figured out how to package Crum's snack food. Earl Wise owned a grocery store in Pennsylvania. He noticed that a lot of his potatoes weren't going to last much longer. So he made potato chips and sold them in paper bags. Customers loved them. When someone invented an automatic potato-peeling machine in 1925, Wise was happy. Then he could make lots of potato chips. By 1930 he was selling them in stronger cellophane bags. The Wise brand became the first packaged potato chips.

This is the bag Wise potato chips used in the 1960s.

WISE potato chips
NET WT. 1/2 OZ. AVOIR.
WISE POTATO CHIP CO., BERWICK, PA., SUBSIDIARY OF THE BORDEN CO., ST. AUGUSTINE, FLA.
5¢

George Crum, who was of African and Native American descent, stands in front of the restaurant he opened after inventing the potato chip.

GEO. CRUM

Did Johnny Appleseed Really Plant Apple Trees All Over the United States?

YES—OVER A LARGE PART OF THE UNITED STATES, ANYWAY. Johnny Appleseed was the nickname of John Chapman. He was born in Massachusetts in 1774. When he was about twenty-six years old, Chapman decided to head west. Many young men were doing the same thing. Most of them were pioneers building new towns in the wilderness. But Chapman wasn't interested in building a town. He wanted to plant thousands of apple trees.

When John Chapman reached Pennsylvania, he started collecting apple seeds. He got them at mills where people pressed apples to make apple cider. As he traveled westward, he planted his seeds. He left some of them to grow into trees right where he planted them. He would dig up some saplings after two years. Then he would sell the young trees or give them away. His trees gave early pioneers and Native Americans a source of food.

Although Chapman was a kind and gentle man, he probably startled a lot of adults and kids with his appearance. Chapman's hair was long and flowing, and his feet were bare. His pants looked worn out. And instead of a shirt, he wore a sack that was made to hold coffee beans.

Did You Know

When you plant the seeds of a fruit tree, the new plants are not exactly like the "mother" plant. To make the new plant true to its "mother," you have to use special cultivation (plant-growing) techniques. But Chapman wanted many types of apple trees to sprout in the wilderness. So he simply planted the seeds in the ground. And with his help, hundreds of new apple varieties spread across the Midwest.

People often feel like napping after a Thanksgiving feast. They may have eaten turkey, gravy, cranberries, stuffing, potatoes, and, oh, a slice or two of pie. But what do those sleepy diners blame almost every time? The turkey. That's because it's a common belief that turkey makes you tired.

Turkey is often the centerpiece at Thanksgiving meals.

It's true that turkey contains tryptophan—and tryptophan can make people sleepy. Tryptophan is a type of amino acid. Amino acids are building blocks for the cells in our bodies. Our bodies use tryptophan to make (among other things) a chemical in the brain that helps us sleep.

But it's probably *not* true that turkey is to blame for Thanksgiving-Day napping. That's because the tryptophan in turkey affects someone only if turkey is all that he or she is eating. And that person would have to eat an awful lot of turkey. Plus, other common foods contain tryptophan too. Beef, chicken, and tofu are among them. So if turkey makes us sleepy, then so should chicken nuggets and hamburgers.

So why do people feel sluggish after the annual Thanksgiving turkey feast? Most doctors and nutrition experts think people eat too much on Thanksgiving. And overeating does make people sleepy.

Are Fortune Cookies Really a Chinese Food?

NOPE. At Chinese restaurants, diners eat hundreds of different dishes. But most of the restaurant goers end their meal the same way—with a crunchy fortune cookie. The diner quickly snaps open the cookie to learn what the future will hold. But wait a sec! We're not talking about restaurants in China. These are restaurants in the United States that serve Chinese food. Most food historians believe the fortune cookie was born in the United States.

So who came up with the idea for these popular cookies? No one is sure. Some historians think the credit belongs to a man named Makoto Hagiwara. In 1914 he was in charge of a garden in San Francisco where people could drink tea. And that year, he supposedly began offering fortune cookies to visitors. But maybe the cookie genius was George Jung. He was a baker and a preacher. According to one story, he invented fortune cookies in 1918 and gave them to poor people. The "fortunes" were quotations from the Bible. Or maybe neither man deserves the credit. At least one food historian thinks fortune cookies were invented in Japan.

Americans loved these crispy cookies and probably didn't give much thought to who the inventor was. Eventually several American companies were making fortune cookies—lots of them. By 2007 Wonton Food Inc. was making 4 million cookies per day for its Golden Bowl brand.

A Cookie Maker Does Not Earn a Fortune in China

In the 1990s, U.S. fortune cookie maker Wonton Foods decided it was time to introduce fortune cookies to China. A year later, the company opened a factory there. But not many Chinese people bought the cookies. One executive at Wonton Foods thought he understood why. The cookies were just too American!

Is a Tomato Really a Fruit?

THE ANSWER DEPENDS ON WHOM YOU ASK. Plant experts think of a tomato as the fruit of a particular type of plant. Dictionaries agree. But most of us treat a tomato like a vegetable. We eat tomatoes in salads and on top of pizzas. We don't usually put them in cakes or in sweet pies, as we do apples and other fruits.

Tomatoes grow from the flower of a plant and contain seeds, just as other fruits do.

If you like pizza, then you probably like tomatoes. Pizza sauce is made with tomatoes!

Why do plant experts say a tomato is a fruit? Because every tomato develops from one of the flowers on a tomato plant. The tomato grows out of a part of the flower called the ovary. And it contains the seeds of the plant. Other fruits grow the same way. An orange grows out of the ovary of one of the flowers on an orange tree.

Tomatoes have something else in common with some other fruit. They contain vitamin C. In fact, people in the United States get most of their vitamin C from tomatoes. Although an orange has much more vitamin C than a tomato, people eat many more tomatoes than oranges. They usually eat tomatoes in cooked form, for example in spaghetti sauce.

Can you guess which people were the first to make a sauce from tomatoes? You're probably guessing Italians. That's a good guess. However, the Aztec people made a sauce from tomatoes and chili peppers in Central America before tomatoes even grew in Europe. So how did Italians find out about tomatoes? When Spanish conquerors arrived in Central America in the 1500s, they saw tomatoes for the first time. The Spanish brought tomato plants back to Europe with them.

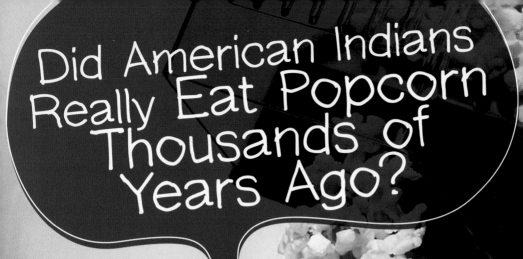

Did American Indians Really Eat Popcorn Thousands of Years Ago?

YES! In 1950 graduate student Herbert Dick found some ancient kernels of popcorn in a cave in New Mexico. Dick could guess what type of corn he had found, because six of the kernels had been popped. And he knew that American Indians ate popcorn by the time European explorers arrived in North America around 1500. Dick was a student of anthropology (the study of humans and their ancient ancestors). So he was very excited about his find.

Dick gave the corn kernels to Paul Mangelsdorf, an expert on corn. Mangelsdorf placed ten of the unpopped kernels on a moist paper towel in a special dish. After two days, he dropped the popcorn into hot oil. Sure enough, they popped. Just how old were those ancient kernels? Scientists agreed they could have been at least 1,700 years old! The find showed that people had been eating popcorn longer than anyone had known.

Although popcorn has existed in North America since ancient times, it took awhile for it to catch on outside of the Southwest. Most historians think true popcorn didn't spread to the land east of the Mississippi River until the early 1800s. It became wildly popular in the late 1830s, when one of the first contraptions for popping popcorn was invented. This early popcorn popper was a simple wire basket with a long handle. The handle made it possible for someone to pop popcorn over an open fire without burning his or her hands. Soon more advanced popcorn poppers were designed. And even more people began enjoying popcorn.

The Big Bang

Popcorn is made by roasting popcorn kernels with a little fat, heating them with dry heat, or popping them in a microwave oven. Each kernel is covered by a hard shell called a pericarp. When the kernel cooks, the starch inside the pericarp fills with steam. The kernel builds up so much pressure that it explodes with a pop. The pericarp splits and turns inside out, allowing the starchy part to expand. And there it is—a perfectly airy yet crunchy snack. All it needs is a light drizzle of butter and a hungry mouth.

Is It True That Fats in Food Are Always Bad for You?

NO! You would be in trouble if you didn't eat any fat. It acts as a fuel that gives you energy. Your body also uses fats to make hormones. These chemical messengers help parts of your body to communicate with one another. Kids and teens need fats more than adults do. That's because their bodies are still growing and developing.

Can you identify which of these foods have bad fats and which have good fats?

The fats that are best for you are called unsaturated fats. They are oils that come from vegetables, nuts, and seeds. These fats are liquid at room temperature. Corn oil, walnut oil, and sunflower oil are all unsaturated fats.

Saturated fats can harm your body if you eat a lot of them. These fats are usually solid at room temperature. Butter is a saturated fat, and so is the fatty part of a steak. Most saturated fats come from animals. But a few come from tropical plants, such as coconut oil and palm kernel oil.

What's so bad about saturated fats? They can encourage your body to build up too much cholesterol. This waxy substance is useful for building the walls of your cells and for making some types of hormones. But having too much cholesterol in your body can eventually lead to heart disease.

What's an easy way to get more good fats in your diet—and to keep the bad fats out? Try eating some nuts. They contain mainly good fats. So do avocados, olives, salmon, and trout. But pass on fried or breaded meats, doughnuts, and cupcakes. These contain lots of saturated fats.

Were Chocolate Chip Cookies Once Called Toll House Cookies?

YEP. The name—and the cookie—came from Ruth Wakefield. She owned the Toll House Inn, in Whitman, Massachusetts, in the early 1930s. The inn had begun its life about two centuries earlier as a toll house, where a toll keeper lived. He collected tolls, or fees for using the road, from people traveling to or from Boston.

One day, while making plain butter cookies, Wakefield had an idea. She chopped up a Nestlé chocolate bar and dropped it into the batter. This was a new way to bake with chocolate. At that time, when a baker wanted to add chocolate to dough, she melted it first. Whitman discovered that when she baked the dough with the chopped-up chocolate, the chocolate didn't melt—it just softened. And after the cookies cooled, the chocolate pieces gave them a nice, crunchy texture.

Wakefield's recipe was published in a Boston newspaper. Toll House cookies soon became very popular. The Nestlé company realized it was selling a lot more chocolate bars—which bakers chopped up to mix into dough. In 1939 the company decided to give bakers a helping hand. Nestlé started making chocolate chips. And on every package, they printed Ruth Wakefield's recipe.

The $250 Cookie Recipe

Another story about chocolate chip cookies has been circulating for decades. According to the story, a woman and her daughter ate lunch in the restaurant of an expensive department store. They loved the chocolate chip cookies there. So the woman asked for the recipe. Their server said they were welcome to the recipe, but that they would be charged two-fifty. The woman assumed that meant $2.50, and she agreed to pay. But the store added $250 to her lunch bill. The woman paid the bill, but she was furious. She got her revenge by giving out free copies of the recipe to everyone she could think of. When the Internet expanded in the 1990s, this story spread like wildfire. But it's completely false.

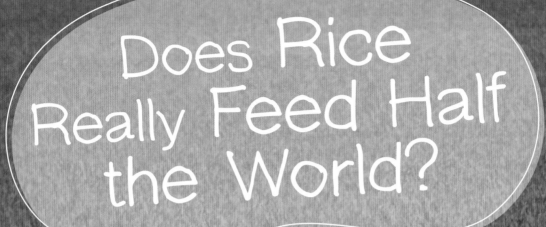

Does Rice Really Feed Half the World?

YES! Rice is a main food for about half the world's population. People enjoy it in different ways. Japanese people love sticky rice and fish rolled up together in a ribbon of dried seaweed. People in Thailand, Cambodia, and Vietnam often eat rice noodles, made from powdered rice. In the Caribbean, Central America, and parts of the United States, people enjoy the winning combination of rice and beans.

Thousands of varieties of rice grow throughout the world. This grain comes in a rainbow of colors, including brown, red, purple, and black. The texture varies too. In China, Taiwan, and Egypt, people like sticky rice. In southern Asia, dry and flaky rice is preferred.

No matter how it's eaten, rice is grown in flooded fields. Grassy-looking rice plants are covered with about 2 to 4 inches (5 to 10 centimeters) of water until they're ready to harvest. After the rice is harvested, the hulls (outer coverings) are removed from the grains. A brown layer called the bran also surrounds each white grain of rice. If the bran is left on, the rice is called brown rice. Brown rice contains vitamins and protein and is very nutritious. To get white rice, the bran is removed. Unfortunately, a lot of the vitamins and protein disappear along with the bran. But rice is a good source of energy no matter what color it is.

A woman works in a rice field in Vietnam.

Did You Know?

In homes all over the city of New Orleans, Louisiana, many people still sit down to a meal of red beans and rice (left) every Monday. Why Monday? It's an old tradition. Monday used to be washday. Cooks liked to make something that could bubble gently on the stove while they did the laundry. Red beans and rice was just the ticket.

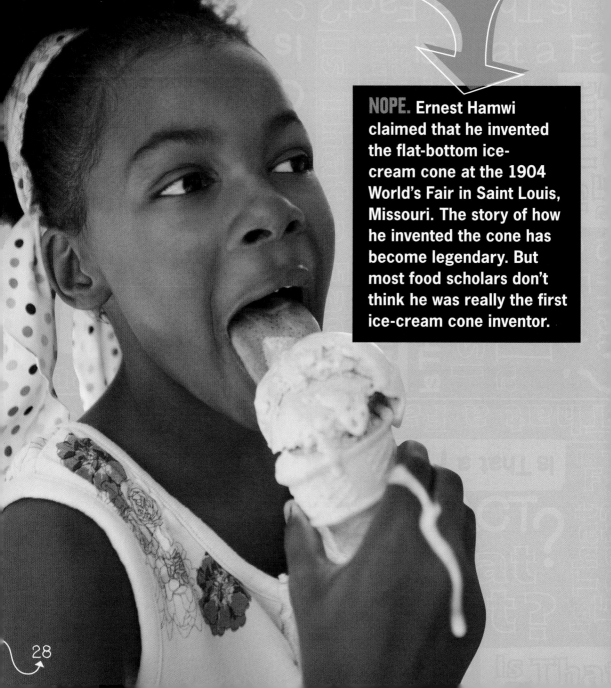

Was the Ice-Cream Cone Really Invented at the Saint Louis World's Fair?

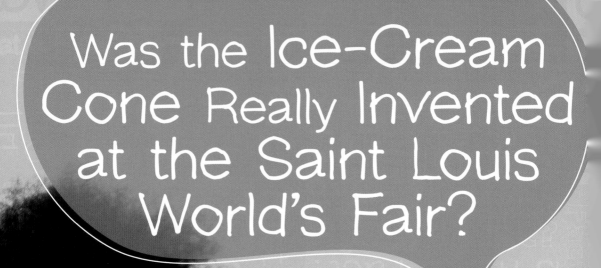

NOPE. Ernest Hamwi claimed that he invented the flat-bottom ice-cream cone at the 1904 World's Fair in Saint Louis, Missouri. The story of how he invented the cone has become legendary. But most food scholars don't think he was really the first ice-cream cone inventor.

Here's how the story goes. Hamwi went to the fair to set up a waffle stand. He sold waffles all day to customers from his stand. Next to him was an ice-cream vendor who had a problem. He'd run out of bowls and couldn't serve ice cream to his customers. That's when Hamwi said he came up with an idea. He started rolling up waffles in which the ice cream could be served. The ice-cream cone was born.

Hamwi really did sell waffles at the fair. And he really did make them into containers for ice cream. But he probably wasn't the one who came up with the idea. An Italian man named Italo Marchiony most likely invented the ice-cream cone. Marchiony sold flavored ices (similar to snow cones or sorbet) from a cart in New York City. He started out serving the ices in glass cups. But the cups were expensive. So Marchiony shaped a pastry into a cup with a flat bottom and slanted sides. He served ices in those cups instead. He received a patent for his invention in 1903—a year before the Saint Louis World's Fair.

The Saint Louis World's Fair

The Saint Louis World's Fair (right) was organized to honor the hundredth anniversary of the Louisiana Purchase. In this 1803 land deal, Thomas Jefferson purchased a vast area of land in the midwestern United States. The fair's official name was the Louisiana Purchase Exposition.

Twenty million people came to the fair. They wandered through exhibits from forty-five states and fifty countries. Many sampled foods they had never seen before. These foods included hamburgers, iced tea, bread sliced by a machine, and—of course—Hamwi's waffle ice-cream cones.

Is It True That Organic Food Is Always Best for the Environment?

IT DEPENDS WHOM YOU ASK. You may have to decide this one for yourself!

ORGANIC FRUIT

?

LOCAL FRUIT

If you want to choose food that is best for the environment, you'll have a lot to think about. Let's start with the way fruits and vegetables are grown. Most of them are grown on large farms. The farmers use fertilizer to help plants grow. They also spray plants with powerful pesticides to keep insects from destroying the plants. Chemicals in the fertilizers and pesticides pollute the soil and nearby rivers and streams. Eventually these chemicals flow into the ocean and pollute it too. They can also hurt animals other than the pests they're meant for.

Organic farms don't use harmful pesticides and fertilizers. So it's a no-brainer, right? Organic food is obviously better. Not so fast. Environmental experts agree that organic food is often best. But some experts believe it's best to buy food that's grown locally. When you buy organic blueberries from Chile, the blueberries travel thousands of miles by airplane. That airplane pollutes the air much more than a farmer's truck delivering fruit to a nearby market. So the buy-local folks would advise you to buy only blueberries grown nearby, during the local growing season. Then you'll buy food with lower food miles.

Other researchers say you should stop counting food miles. You'll do more

These bags of fertilizer are being shipped to farms to help crops grow. Some people are concerned that some chemicals in the fertilizers are hurting the planet.

for the environment if you just eat less beef and pork. For one thing, cattle and pigs pass a lot of gas into the air. Pigs are big belchers! The animals' poop produces gas too. One of the gases produced is methane, which contributes to global warming—the recent increase in Earth's average surface temperature. (Possible dangers of this warming include droughts, food shortages, and coastal flooding.) In addition, larger farm animals eat a lot of grain. About one-third of the grain that is grown around the world goes to feed animals. And that grain is usually produced with the help of fertilizers and pesticides.

Who said Earth-friendly grocery shopping was simple?

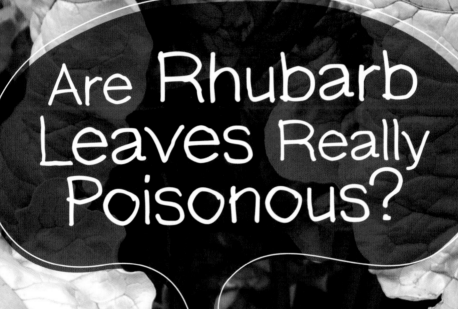

Are Rhubarb Leaves Really Poisonous?

YEP. Rhubarb is a plant with thick, celery-like stalks and very large leaves. In fact, the leaves are so big that when you see a clump growing out of the ground, you may not even notice the reddish stems. It's the stems and not the leaves that cooks use. You won't see any leaves in strawberry rhubarb pie, rhubarb crisp, or any other tasty sweet made with rhubarb.

Rhubarb leaves contain oxalic acid, which is a poisonous substance. It would take a lot of rhubarb leaves to kill someone, though. A woman who weighs 130 pounds (59 kilograms) would have to eat 10 pounds (4.5 kg) of rhubarb leaves. If she ate only a pound or two (0.5 to 0.9 kg)—still a lot—the leaves wouldn't kill her. But they would make her sick, and they might damage her kidneys.

During World War I (1914–1918), some people in Britain learned about poisonous rhubarb leaves the hard way. The war created food shortages. People were looking for cheap, filling food. Rhubarb leaves were suggested as a replacement for vegetables that were scarce. Recipes for rhubarb leaves started popping up. But the dishes made people sick, and a few people died.

The stems of the rhubarb plant are edible. You can use them to make delicious rhubarb pie and rhubarb crumble.

But don't let those nasty leaves scare you away from eating the stems. There are lots of yummy ways to enjoy rhubarb stems. Try rhubarb crisp, with its crunchy oat and brown sugar topping, or strawberry-rhubarb sauce on top of vanilla ice cream!

Rhubarb on the Radio

In the early 1900s, there was no such thing as television. People listened to dramatic stories on the radio for entertainment. When the rumbling sound of an angry crowd was needed, the actors mumbled "rhubarb" over and over.

Did the Pilgrims Really Eat Cranberry Sauce and Sweet Potatoes at Their Thanksgiving Feast?

NOPE. Cranberries *were* a traditional food for the Wampanoag people, who shared in the Pilgrims' feast. In fact, American Indians in what is now the northeastern United States had been eating cranberries long before the Pilgrims came to North America. But we don't have any reason to believe that the berries were part of the feast. And as for sweet potatoes, they were rare in New England in 1621, when the Thanksgiving feast took place. Until the 1800s, sweet potatoes were mostly grown in Virginia, Georgia, and North and South Carolina.

So what did the Pilgrims feast on at the Plymouth Colony? We're not sure. The only record we have of the Pilgrims' first Thanksgiving feast is a letter written by the Pilgrim Edward Winslow. According to Winslow, Governor William Bradford sent four Pilgrims to hunt for wild fowl for the feast. The fowl could have been geese, swans, ducks, pigeons, and—you guessed it—turkey. But we'll never know for sure. Historians also think the Wampanoag and their leader, Massasoit, brought venison (deer meat) to the meal.

Although we don't know the details about that Thanksgiving feast, we do know that it wasn't a rushed event. The feasting went on for three days.

This painting from the 1930s shows the Pilgrims feasting with the Wampanoag in 1621.

The "First Thanksgiving Feast" Wasn't the First

The Pilgrims weren't the first colonists from England to celebrate a thanksgiving in North America. When they arrived in Plymouth in 1620, there was already an English settlement in Jamestown, Virginia. And the settlers there had already observed at least one thanksgiving celebration by 1619. In fact, in the 1600s and 1700s, the governors and church ministers of the colonies proclaimed thousands of thanksgivings. Some celebrated harvests or much-needed rain. Others celebrated military victories. The Thanksgiving Day feast we celebrate every November doesn't really have an authentic historical tie with the Pilgrims' feast of 1621. That connection is a myth.

Do People Really Run Pancake Races in England?

YES. In Olney, England, people have been flipping over their pancake race for more than five hundred years! No one is absolutely certain when or why this custom began. But the standard explanation goes like this:

wearing her apron and carrying her skillet with a pancake in it! The women in Olney have been running in a pancake race on Shrove Tuesday ever since.

The pancake race is very short. It lasts for about a minute. But the rules are strictly followed. The contestants must be women. They have to wear aprons and scarves on their heads, just as women did long ago. And they have to carry a skillet with a pancake in it. When the winner reaches the end of the 415-yard (379-meter) racecourse, she has to toss her pancake to flip it in the skillet. Although the rules are taken seriously, people laugh and have a good time.

It all began just before Lent in 1445. In many Christian traditions, Lent is a period of forty days when people get ready for the Easter holiday. Lent is a serious time. In England, people go to church on Shrove Tuesday, the day before Lent begins. On that day in 1445, the church bells rang in the town of Olney. Church was about to start. One woman was making pancakes when she heard the bells. She raced to the church so she wouldn't be late—still

An American Challenger

Olney's race inspired the people in the town of Liberal, Kansas, to start their own pancake race in 1940. Ten years later, the town decided to challenge the winner of Olney's race to see who ran the fastest. Both races start at 11:55 A.M. in their respective time zones. Every year, the winner of the Olney race has to wait to see if the winner of the Kansas race made better time. That's because the time zone of Liberal, Kansas, is six hours behind the time zone of Olney.

GLOSSARY

amino acid: one of the building blocks of cells in your body

anthropology: the study of humans and their ancient ancestors

bran: the outer covering of a grain, such as rice or wheat

cholesterol: a waxy substance that your body uses for building the walls of cells and making some types of hormones

dissolve: to seem to disappear when mixed with water

fertilizer: something used on soil to help crops or other types of plants grow well

fowl: a type of bird, such as a duck or a goose

harvest: to gather a crop

hormone: a chemical messenger that helps parts of your body communicate with one another

hull: the outer covering of a fruit or a seed, such as a grain of rice

methane: a type of gas that has no odor or color. Methane gas contributes to global warming.

molecule: the smallest part of a substance that has all of its properties

organic: produced without chemicals, such as fertilizers or pesticides

ovary: the part of a flowering plant in which the seeds form

patent: a legal document that gives only an inventor the right to make or sell his or her invention

pericarp: the hard shell that covers a popcorn kernel

pesticide: a chemical used to kill insects and other farm and garden pests

pollute: to make the land, air, or water dirty

sapling: a young tree

saturated fat: fat that is solid at room temperature. Most saturated fats come from animal products.

tryptophan: a type of amino acid that does a number of different jobs in your body, including helping you sleep

unsaturated fat: fats from seeds, nuts, and vegetables that are liquid at room temperature

vapor: a gas formed from water or another substance

venison: deer meat

SELECTED BIBLIOGRAPHY

Davidson, Alan. *The Oxford Companion to Food*. Oxford: Oxford University Press, 1999.

Martin, Andrew. "If It's Fresh and Local, Is It Always Greener?" *New York Times*. December 9, 2007. http://www .nytimes.com/2007/12/09/business/ yourmoney/09feed.html (May 4, 2010).

Smith, Andrew F. *The Turkey: An American Story*. Chicago: University of Illinois Press, 2006.

————., ed. *The Oxford Companion to American Food and Drink*. New York: Oxford University Press, 2007.

Trager, James. *The Food Chronology: A Food Lover's Compendium of Events and Anecdotes, from Prehistory to the Present*. New York: Henry Holt, 1995.

Zanini De Vita, Oretta. *Encyclopedia of Pasta*. Translated by Maureen B. Fant. Berkeley, CA: University of California Press, 2009.

FURTHER READING

D'Aluisio, Faith. *What the World Eats*. Berkeley, CA: Tricycle Press, 2008. This book is filled with information and colorful photographs of twenty-five families in twenty-one countries and the food they eat.

Doeden, Matt. *Eat Right! How You Can Make Good Food Choices*. Minneapolis: Lerner Publications Company, 2009. Learn how to give your body the fuel it needs to run properly. Become an expert at reading food labels.

Everyday Mysteries
http://www.loc.gov/rr/scitech/mysteries
Check out this site to find the answers to some interesting questions about food, nutrition, farming, crops, and more.

The First Thanksgiving: You Are the Historian
http://www.plimoth.org/education/ olc/index_js2.html
This website, sponsored by the Plimoth Plantation, takes you on a journey to discover what really happened on the first Thanksgiving Day at the Plymouth Colony. Get ready to be a historian and do some detective work!

Micucci, Charles. *The Life and Times of Corn*. Boston: Houghton Mifflin Books for Children, 2009. Find out more about popcorn and other types of corn in this book, which features funny cartoons and watercolor illustrations.

Taylor, Gaylia. *George Crum and the Saratoga Chip*. New York: Lee and Low, 2006. This book tells the story of George Crum's life, including his delicious invention—potato chips.

INDEX

ACKNOWLEDGMENTS
The images in this book are used with the permission of:
© iStockphoto.com/Manuela Weschke, p. 1; © iStockphoto.
com/Uyen Le, pp. 2 (bottom), 18–19; © iStockphoto.com/
Kelly Cline, pp. 2, (top), 4 (top), 13 (inset), 14–15; © Sean
Prior/Shutterstock Images, pp. 3 (top), 24; © CREATISTA/
Shutterstock Images, pp. 3 (bottom), 34 (bottom);
© Vladimir Surkov/Dreamstime.com, pp. 4 (bottom), 22 (top);
© Gustavo Fadel/Shutterstock Images, p. 5; © kilukilu/
Shutterstock Images, pp. 6–7; © Friedrich Saurer/Alamy,
p. 7 (inset); © iStockphoto.com/LamplighterSDV, pp. 9–10;
© John Sims/Fresh Food Images/Photolibrary, p. 9 (inset);
© George Doyle & Ciaran Griffin/Stockbyte/Getty Images,
pp. 10–11; © Courtesy of the Saratoga Springs History
Museum p. 11 (top), (bottom); © 2011 Wise Foods, Inc. All
Rights Reserved, p. 11 (middle); © David Toy/Alamy,
pp. 12–13; © Radius Images/Alamy, p. 15 (inset); © Melissa
Raimondi/Dreamstime.com, pp. 16–17; © Mchudo/
Dreamstime.com, p. 18 (inset); © Monkey Business Images/
Dreamstime.com, p. 19 (inset); © Photolibrary RF/Glow
Images, p. 20; © Sikth/Dreamstime.com, p. 21; © AGfoto/
Shutterstock Images, p. 22 (bottom); © Ivonne Wierink/
Dreamstime.com, p. 23 (top); © Sandra Caldwell/Shutterstock
Images, p. 23 (bottom); © Todd Strand/Independent Picture
Service, p. 25 (all); © Megapress/Alamy, pp. 26–27; © Rita
Mass/FoodPix/Getty Images, p. 26 (inset); © Blend Images/
SuperStock, p. 28; Library of Congress pp. 29 (LC-
USZ62-48207), 35 (bottom, LC-USZC4-4961); © Phase4
Photography/Shutterstock Images, pp. 30–31; © Jung
Yeon-Je/AFP/Getty Images, p. 31 (top); © iStockphoto.com/
Eric Isselée, p. 31 (bottom); © Lilac Mountain/Shutterstock
Images, pp. 32–33; © Europress/Profimedia International
s.r.o./Alamy, p. 33 (top); © Giliane E. Mansfeldt/courtesy of
the Minnesota History Center/Saint Olaf College, p. 33
(bottom); © Don Bendickson/Shutterstock Images, p. 34
(top); © vita khorzhevska/Shutterstock Images, p. 35 (top);
© Robert Estall/Robert Estall photo agency/Alamy,
pp. 36–37; © Rupert Horrox/Dorling Kindersley/Getty Images,
p. 37 (inset).

Front Cover: © iStockphoto.com/winterling (bag of potato
chips); © iStockphoto.com/Manuela Weschke (cook).

Lerner Publications Company
A division of Lerner Publishing Group, Inc.
241 First Avenue North
Minneapolis, MN 55401 U.S.A.

Website address: www.lernerbooks.com

Library of Congress Cataloging-in-Publication Data

Kops, Deborah.
    Were potato chips really invented by an angry chef? :
and other questions about food / by Deborah Kops.
        p.   cm. — (Is that a fact?)
    Includes bibliographical references and index.
    ISBN 978–0–7613–6099–5 (lib. bdg. : alk. paper)
    1. Food—Miscellanea—Juvenile literature. I. Title.
TX355.K675 2011
641.3—dc22   2010027976

Manufactured in the United States of America
1 – CG – 12/31/10